BECAUSE YOU _ALMOST_ CAN'T LIVE WITHOUT IT!

WHAT ELSE CAN I DO WITH MY MICROWAVE?

Also by Ruth Spear
WHAT CAN I DO WITH MY MICROWAVE?
THE EAST HAMPTON COOKBOOK
COOKING FISH AND SHELLFISH
THE CLASSIC VEGETABLE COOKBOOK
LOW FAT AND LOVING IT

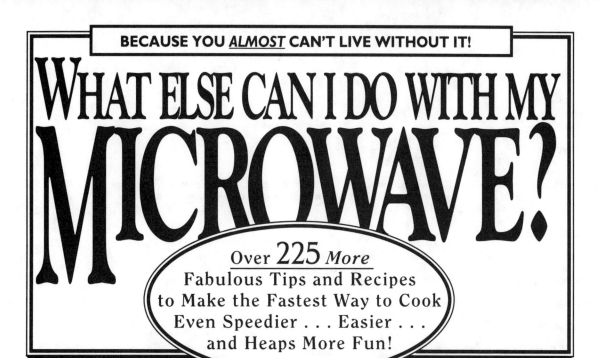

BECAUSE YOU _ALMOST_ CAN'T LIVE WITHOUT IT!

WHAT ELSE CAN I DO WITH MY MICROWAVE?

Over 225 _More_
Fabulous Tips and Recipes
to Make the Fastest Way to Cook
Even Speedier . . . Easier . . .
and Heaps More Fun!

RUTH SPEAR
best-selling author of _What Can I Do with My Microwave?_

A DELL TRADE PAPERBACK

A DELL TRADE PAPERBACK

Published by
Dell Publishing
a division of
Bantam Doubleday Dell Publishing Group, Inc.
1540 Broadway
New York, New York 10036

The trademark Dell ® is registered in the U.S. Patent and Trademark Office.

ISBN: 0-440-50508-9

Printed in the United States of America

Published simultaneously in Canada

September 1993

10   9   8   7   6   5   4   3   2   1

SEM

To my mother-in-law,
Esther Spear,
always a source
of enthusiasm and support

Grateful acknowledgment is made for permission to use the following recipes which are adapted or derived from the sources below.

Glazed Walnuts, *Quick Harvest,* Pat Baird, Prentice Hall Press, NY, 1991

Party Snack Mix, Hot Spiced Cider, *Easy Livin' Microwave Cooking,* Karen Kangas Dwyer, St. Martin's Press, NY, 1989

Baked Apple with Crème Anglaise, adapted from *Sweet Times,* Dorie Greenspan, Wm. Morrow & Co., NY, 1991

CONTENTS

INTRODUCTION

When I wrote *What Can I Do with My Microwave?* in 1988, I was still experiencing the thrill of having recently acquired a microwave (I had been a hard-nosed holdout), and while I was excited by the many small ways this wonderful machine simplified my life, I certainly was not ready to commit myself to cooking with it in any meaningful way. My philosophy, which I would tell anyone at the drop of a hat, was to consider it part of my *batterie de cuisine*, just another kitchen tool, albeit a very versatile one. Experienced cooks often resist the idea of changing everything they've learned to use a new cooking method, even though the advantages in time savings and ease of preparation are apparent. I know—I was one of them. Now that I have absorbed those changes into my cooking lifestyle, I find myself increasingly and instinctively modifying and enhancing as I become more and more familiar with this wonderful machine.

Some things I still resist; I don't own a browning gadget, because if it's direct heat that's needed, that's what my food gets. I wouldn't roast a chicken in the microwave, either, because I love what comes out of my oven. I know it's possible. I just see no reason to change. On the other hand, the idea of *not* having to light my stove on a hot summer day to poach chicken breasts for our picnic chicken salad appeals to me greatly.

I'm hoping my readers will have grown with me. Now that I'm comfortable with basic microwave principles, I've become more creative, and invite you to do so, too. I see little point in trying to convert a recipe unless the time differential is significant or the foolproof factor important enough to make the change worthwhile. There are, however, literally dozens, if not hundreds, of things you can do in the microwave, which are cleaner, easier, and faster than if cooked conventionally, and usually end up tasting better, too. The fruit compote my husband is so fond of, which we use for dessert and as a relish with meats or chicken, is a snap in the microwave. So is Crème Anglaise (p. 83) or thin custard sauce, which makes a special dessert out of practically anything. And imagine a moist, tasty fish dinner (Oriental Flounder Fillets, p. 77) in 5 minutes!

Microwave cooking has its limitations, but often these yield a slightly different but still totally acceptable food. For example, the characteristic smoky taste of the Middle Eastern eggplant appetizer Baba Ghanoush (p. 40), which comes from charring it under the broiler, is missing in the microwave version. But the result is still a good, flavorful dip that has a validity on its own. Especially when it makes entertaining easier.

Some foods actually taste better when made in the microwave. It is a revelation that something as simple as new potatoes, which I adore, have a much better, sweeter flavor and more interesting waxy texture, when made in the microwave, plus there's no pot to wash out. It is safe to say that almost no day goes by that my microwave is not in use in some aspect of a meal, heating our morning milk for café au lait, making oatmeal, defrosting and heating broth to cook rice, making cocoa, warming bread.

There are certain preparations that just naturally lend themselves to the microwave, that can at once simplify and enrich your cooking life. They are included in the "minirecipes" in this volume and I hope they will bring you as much pleasure as they do me.

Many of these little recipes will serve as models to enable you to create recipes of your own. For example, once you understand how to do chicken breasts in the microwave, you may use the technique to adapt a personal favorite chicken breast dish. The same holds true for fish fillets. Many busy cooks find themselves skimping on serving vegetables to their families because of the pots, pans, and cooking time involved. The microwave makes serving fresh vegetables a snap and the bonus is that it conserves a maximum amount of nutrients besides. Baked potatoes (both sweet and white), new potatoes, corn on the cob, asparagus, broccoli, and baked squash of all kinds are vegetables I regularly cook in the microwave.

Speaking of health, one of the most interesting and valuable aspects of microwave cooking, apart from its time-saving nature, is the way in which it allows one to cook a greater number of foods with little or no added oil or butter—a boon in these fat-conscious times. Note that something as simple as a scrambled egg (p. 61) can be made with no added fat and still emerge fluffy and moist. Best of all, because it is so easy to make something healthful to eat when hunger strikes, you are less likely to pig out on high-fat, calorie-dense snack food.

—RUTH SPEAR

GUIDELINES

These recipes were tested in a 650-watt microwave. If your oven has a higher or lower wattage you may want to adjust cooking times accordingly.

All cooking vessels called for, especially those of glass, should be "microwave safe." To avoid repetition, **MWS** in the text means a **microwave-safe** vessel. All plastic wrap should be microwave safe, as well.

All these recipes were tested in an oven with a revolving turntable. If you do not have one, rotate the food container once while cooking.

Microwave ovens range from between 450 and 700 watts of cooking power, with 600–700 watts the most popular. When a range of cooking times is given, use the shorter time for an oven of higher wattage. It's a good idea to jot down the times of frequently cooked foods for quick referral.

Below are the power equivalents for settings used in this book: the percentages refer to the percentage of full power the oven uses. The first figure is applicable to newer and/or larger machines. The second figure may apply to older ovens with fewer options, or to smaller machines. If you are not sure about your machine, check the manufacturer's booklet.

HIGH = 100%
MEDIUM HIGH = 70%–80%
MEDIUM = 50%–70%
MEDIUM LOW (DEFROST) = 30%–50%
LOW = 10%–20%

Powers are given by name in this book because percentages can vary from manufacturer to manufacturer. Generally speaking, more delicate foods, eggs for example, are best cooked at lower powers.

MICROWAVE BASICS

UTENSILS FOR YOUR MICROWAVE

While housewares stores offer a dizzying array of microwave cooking utensils and accessories, I've found that a few choice ones are all you really need.

Pyrex glass ovenware is ideal for the microwave, and the new designs have responded to the particular requirements of the microwave as well. Measuring cups, for example, in which you can heat and cook many liquids, have been redesigned with substantial headroom to avoid boil-overs.

My favorites are:

The 8-inch/21 cm. cake dish, which, because of its generous 2-inch depth, straight sides, and convenient handles is endlessly useful. The broad, flat bottom makes it easy to arrange food to be microwaved; the shape also exposes more food to the microwaves and allows it to cook, reducing stirring to a minimum.

Note that the cover of the 2-quart Pyrex casserole fits this dish.
1-quart Pyrex casserole with cover
Porcelain soufflé dishes of varying sizes
Pyrex "custard" cups—6-ounce size
2-quart Pyrex casserole with cover
Round Pyrex pie plate
1-cup Pyrex glass measure
2-cup Pyrex glass measure
4-cup Pyrex glass measure
8-cup Pyrex glass measure (This size is extremely useful for heating large quantities of soups and liquids without risking their boiling over. Also ideal for making soups.)
2-quart MWS round ring for baking
A microwave rack for hamburgers, bacon, drying fruits
A browning dish if you want to brown meats in the oven (I don't)
Plain porcelain soufflé dishes of all sizes make excellent microwave dishes, and they can go to the table as well.

MICROWAVE SAFETY AND GENERAL CARE

How Safe Is My Microwave?

Microwave ovens are safe when used as directed. Don't be afraid to watch your food through the oven door as it cooks. The finely perforated metal screen imbedded in the door prevents the escape of microwave energy, yet permits you to check food as you cook.

1 MICROWAVE LEAKAGE
If your microwave is in good repair and you follow the instructions in the manual, leakage should be of no concern. By law, all ovens have a double interlock preventing their use with the door open, which would present the only problem.

For added peace of mind, take these precautions: Inspect the door gasket occasionally, to make sure it hasn't corroded or gotten dirty. Keep it clean by wiping occasionally with a cloth dampened with warm water; don't use harsh abrasives. Don't allow soil or cleaner residue to accumulate on sealing surfaces.

Don't try to use a damaged oven, particularly if the hinges, latches, or seals seem broken.

Inexpensive radiation leakage checking devices are available at many supermarkets, but these devices are heat sensitive and can occasionally give inaccurate readings. On the whole, they are not reliable.

If you are concerned about leakage even though your oven is in good operating condition, just stay a foot or two away from it while it is in operation.

CLEANING AND CARE

2 EXTERIOR
The outside of most microwave ovens is made of laminated plastic and metal. Clean with mild soap and water and dry with a soft towel. Do not use any harsh or abrasive cleaner.

3 INTERIOR
Cleaning the interior is easy because no heat is generated that will bake onto the surface food that has spilled or spattered. To clean the interior surfaces, simply wipe with a soft cloth and warm water. Grease will respond to a mild soap; stubborn stains can be sprinkled with dry baking soda and wiped with a damp sponge. Rinse thoroughly with warm water.

4 DOOR
Wipe window on both sides with a cloth dampened with mild soap and warm water.

5 TOUCH CONTROL PANEL
If this becomes soiled, open the oven door before wiping, and use a cloth dampened with warm water only. Avoid using excess water and do not scrub or use any kind of chemical cleaner. Do not spray any cleaner on the touch pads.

DOS AND DON'TS THAT BEAR REPEATING

6 DO NOT operate your microwave when it is empty. If it is new to you and you want to become familiar with its features, practice operating the oven with 1 cup of water inside.

7 DO NOT cook eggs in the shell in your microwave. Built-up pressure will cause the eggs to explode and can cause serious damage to eyes and face.

8 **DO** remember to pierce the yolk of a poached or sunnyside-up egg when cooking it in the microwave. The yolk is held by a membrane which causes the same explosion as the shell.

9 **DO NOT** heat oil or fat for deep-fat frying in the microwave. It can cause a fire.

10 **DO NOT** pop corn in a regular paper bag in the microwave, because the bag could ignite from the high temperature of the kernels. Use only specially packaged microwave-safe bags or a special microwave popper.

11 **DO NOT** heat popcorn longer than the package instructions recommend; if all the corn has popped and the oven is still on, with nothing left to "cook," damage to the oven may result. Do not attempt to reheat unpopped kernels.

12 **DO NOT** remove the turntable when popping corn.

13 DO NOT prepare foods for canning in the microwave; harmful bacteria may not be destroyed.

14 DO check your oven manufacturer's instruction manual if you and it are new to each other.

15 DO keep your oven clean. (See Cleaning and Care.)

MORE MICROWAVE BASICS

16 STANDING TIME
Since microwaved foods continue to cook after they are out of the oven, **standing time** can make a big difference in the results of the food you cook. Standing time is simply the time that food continues to cook as the vibrating molecules slow down. Standing time may last from one to several minutes depending on the food; some need virtually none at all. In general, foods larger in weight or size and/or those that have a relatively long cooking time need longer standing times. Standing time can take place in the oven or on a flat, heat-resistant surface.

17 STARTING TEMPERATURE
Very cold or frozen foods will take longer to heat through and heat evenly than those at room temperature. Take this into consideration when estimating reheating times.

18 VENTING
A food generally covered in conventional cooking should be covered in the microwave, to retain moist heat and prevent evaporation. But be sure to vent the cover or wrap. To vent, completely cover the dish with plastic wrap, then fold back one corner. This prevents steam buildup that can cause burns upon uncovering and also eliminates the possibility of plastic melting onto your food. Remove covers and peel off plastic wrap **away** from your face.

19 COVERING
Although there is little evaporation during microwave cooking, a cover holds in steam which tenderizes food. It also keeps it moist and shortens cooking time. Remove covers carefully; steam can cause burns.

If your instructions say to cover a casserole that has no cover of its own, use a **tight** (unvented) cover of plastic wrap.

A loose casserole cover will allow some steam to escape. You can make it fit tighter by placing a sheet of wax paper between casserole and lid.

20 TURNTABLES

Some microwave ovens have a built-in rotating turntable which rotates the food for more even exposure to microwave energy. It eliminates the need to manually rotate food during cooking.

If a turntable is part of your oven, always leave it in place. Using your oven without it will produce uneven cooking. If your oven does not have a built-in turntable, consider purchasing one.

21 WAX PAPER

Sometimes instructions call for covering a food with wax paper. This forms a loose cover similar to "partial covering" in conventional cooking. Use it to hold in heat, to speed cooking and prevent spatter with foods that do not need steam to tenderize.

22 FOOD ARRANGEMENT

Always try to place food in a ring position in the microwave, with thicker, larger food around the outside.

23 MOISTURE

Any food that sits directly on the floor of the microwave will collect moisture unless you place it on 2 paper towels, paper napkins, or a paper plate lined with a paper towel.

24 "VENTING" FOOD

Foods with natural coverings such as sausages, potatoes, squash, egg yolks, hot dogs, tomatoes, and some fruits also need to be vented so they do not burst or explode in the oven. To vent, simply prick with the tines of a fork two or three times before cooking.

25 COOKING CONTAINERS

The depth of a container is as important as its capacity. Food in a deeper casserole will take longer to microwave than the same amount of food in the same capacity container that is wider and shallower. The shallow casserole exposes more surface to microwave energy.

26 **Round containers** cook food more evenly and should be used whenever possible in the microwave.

27 **Rotate dishes** in the microwave, either manually or with a turntable. Dishes cook more evenly if rotated either constantly or by you every time you stir or check cooking progress.

28 OVENABLE PAPER
Attractive paper "casseroles" can be used to heat food in any type of oven, and, with certain care, are reusable. They are also freezerproof, which means you can make your own freezer-to-microwave-to-table entrées.

29 RECYCLABLE PAPER
Do not use paper towels, plates, or other utensils made

from recycled paper for microwave cooking. Recycled paper may contain impurities that could cause the paper to ignite during microwaving.

30 PLASTIC
Use any dishwasher-safe plastic containers, MWS plastic wrap, boil-in bags, styrofoam cups. Do not use soft plastics (such as lids), which can melt from hot fat or sugar.

Never reheat foods in disposable plastic containers such as those from tub margarine.

31 GLASS
Use any heat-proof glass, ceramic, china, or pottery. Do not use fine china, lead crystal or glass or porcelain trimmed with metal, such as gold or silver.

32 WOOD, STRAW BASKETS
Use for short-time heating only, and make sure basket has no metal staples.

33 TO SPEED DEFROSTING

When defrosting pouches and packages of foods that cannot be stirred or broken up, flex once or twice to redistribute heat.

34 DIET

Food cooked in the microwave usually has fewer calories than the same dish prepared conventionally, because a minimum of butter or oil is required.

Microwaved food, notably vegetables, retains more nutrients, especially water-soluble vitamins, because less liquid is required in cooking.

QUICK TIPS AND TRICKS

Keep potholders handy. MWS dishes can still become hot because they absorb heat from the hot food they contain. This is especially true when food is cooked tightly covered.

35 TEAR-FREE ONIONS

End those tears! Remove the ends but not the papery skin

of one large yellow onion and microwave on HIGH for 1 minute, before chopping, and see the difference.

36 WARM DOG OR CAT FOOD
Take the chill off half a small can by transferring food to a dish and heating on HIGH for 15 to 20 seconds. Stir before serving.

37 REDUCE LIQUIDS
Place liquid or sauce to be reduced in a large glass measure, allowing head room to avoid boiling over. Cook on HIGH and watch until you have the degree of reduction desired.

38 SCALD MILK
Place 1 cup milk in a 2-cup measure and microwave at HIGH for 2–2½ minutes, or until a thin film forms over top of milk and tiny bubbles form at edge of cup.

39 TOAST NUTS
Spread 1 cup nuts in a shallow MWS glass dish. Microwave on HIGH for 3–4 minutes or until just browned. Stir several times while toasting. Let stand 5 minutes before using.

40 DEFROST BREAD
Defrost a loaf of bread in its plastic bag, removing the metal twist tie and microwaving on HIGH for 50–75 seconds. Let stand 5 minutes to completely defrost.

41 NAIL POLISH
Loosen a stuck cap by microwaving 10 seconds on HIGH. Works for cough syrup bottle tops, too.

42 SOFTEN RAISINS
Soften hard raisins by covering ½–1 cup raisins with water in a 2-cup glass measure and microwaving on HIGH for 2–3 minutes.

43 SOFTEN PEANUT BUTTER
Natural peanut butter hard from the refrigerator can be softened by microwaving on HIGH for 1½ minutes per cup. Don't forget to remove lid first. Stir once if more than 1 cup.

44 SOFTEN SMALL SQUASH
To soften and ease cutting, microwave a 1-pound acorn or other small squash on HIGH for 1½ minutes or just until warm to the touch. Then halve, remove seeds, and proceed with your recipe.

45 PEEL TOMATOES
Slash a light X in the skin of a ripe tomato; microwave on HIGH for 15 seconds to loosen skin.

46 MELTING CHOCOLATE
Make sure dish in which you melt chocolate is dry; moisture can cause white streaks.

47 If you find some dry, hard, nonshiny pieces when you stir microwave-melted chocolate, throw them out—the chocolate is scorched and will not blend well.

48 MELTING BUTTER, MARGARINE
Butter and margarine spatter easily when melting; using a lower power takes a little bit longer but eliminates the extra step of covering.

49 GROUND BEEF
Cook beef to be used in chili and pasta sauce and drain the fat at the same time by placing in a MWS colander set into a casserole.

50 BACON
Use plain white paper towels when microwaving bacon. The color in paper towels may transfer to bacon, especially if it has a high sugar content.

51 POPCORN

Elevate microwaveable popcorn bags on an inverted saucer to allow freer circulation of microwaves; this helps more kernels to pop. If making a quantity, pop only one bag at a time, and let oven cool down for 10–15 minutes between batches.

WARMING AND REHEATING

52 REFRIGERATED VEGETABLES

To reheat 1 cup of refrigerated vegetables, microwave on HIGH for 1½–2½ minutes, covered. Stir after half the time.

53 SLICE OF PIE

To warm a slice of pie, place on plate and heat on HIGH for 30 seconds.

54

Add a scoop of ice cream to a slice of pie to be warmed in the microwave (see above) and it will just soften to perfect eating consistency.

55 REHEAT A DINNER PLATE OF FOOD
Cover with plastic wrap, vent and microwave on MEDIUM-HIGH for 1½–3 minutes.

56 REHEATING MEAT
Never reheat refrigerated, cooked meats on HIGH; they do better on MEDIUM.

57 HEATING SOUP
Mix 1 10-ounce can of condensed soup with 1 can of liquid in a MWS casserole, cover and microwave on HIGH for 5–6 minutes.

58 BAKED GOODS
Wrap rolls or bread to be reheated in a paper towel or napkin to absorb extra moisture during reheating.

59 Baked goods should be heated on HIGH only until warm to the touch. They will be hot and moist inside when served.

60 WARMING BREAD
Bread must be completely wrapped in a paper napkin or towel before heating; if the moisture driven to the surface by microwaving is not absorbed, the bread will be hard as a brick.

61 HEAT TACO SHELLS
To heat precooked, crisp taco shells, place on a paper plate and heat on HIGH for 1–3 minutes, until warm.

62 WARM A CROISSANT
To warm a single frozen croissant, microwave wrapped in a paper towel on MEDIUM-LOW or DEFROST (30%) for 1 minute.

63 FRESH BAGELS

Cut fresh bagels in half, put together and freeze in a double plastic bag. For a snack or breakfast, remove one half, wrap in a paper towel or napkin and microwave on HIGH for 20 seconds. The bagel will be as fresh as just-baked. Then toast or not, as you prefer.

64 LAYERED CASSEROLES

When cooking or reheating layered casseroles which cannot be stirred, such as lasagna, use MEDIUM power (50%) and a longer cooking time, so that center of casserole heats without overcooking outer portions.

QUICK, NO-FUSS MEALS AND SNACKS

65 COCKTAIL PECANS

Place 4 tablespoons butter in a 2-quart rectangular dish. Cook on HIGH for 1 minute or until melted. Add 4 teaspoons Worcestershire sauce and 2 teaspoons Lawry's seasoned salt and stir to blend. Add 1 pound large pecan halves, turn to coat with the butter mixture, and microwave, uncovered, on HIGH for 6–8 minutes, stirring once halfway through cooking. The nuts should be dry and fairly dark at the end. Let cool. These nuts will keep a long time in a tightly covered container.

66 GLAZED WALNUTS

In a 10-inch pie plate, combine 2 cups walnut halves with 1 lightly beaten egg white, tossing so that all nuts are moistened. In a small bowl combine ¼ cup brown sugar with ½ teaspoon ground ginger and ¼ teaspoon each ground cinnamon and cayenne pepper. Sprinkle over nuts, spread out in a single layer and microwave on HIGH, uncovered, for 4–6 minutes or until glaze is bubbling and nuts are heated through, stirring every 2 minutes. Stir again after removing from oven. Let cool about 15 minutes. Nuts will crisp as they cool. Separate any that are stuck together. Store in an airtight container.

67 PARTY SNACK MIX

Combine 1⅓ cups each thin pretzel sticks and salted peanuts with 2 cups each Corn Chex, wheat squares, and rice squares in a 3-quart casserole. In a small bowl, microwave ⅓ cup butter with 2 tablespoons Worcestershire sauce, pour over cereal mix, toss well and microwave on HIGH for 6–7 minutes, or until cereal is coated and crisp, stirring every 2 minutes. Spread out on a paper-towel-lined cookie sheet to cool. Makes 9 cups.

68 TACO CHIPS

Make your own greaseless, salt-free taco chips for dips or nachos. Lightly brush both sides of corn or flour tortillas with canola oil, cut each into 6 triangles, place in a single layer on a flat plate and microwave on HIGH for 2–3 minutes until crisp and lightly browned, turning once. Let cool before serving.

69 ITALIAN SAUSAGE AND PEPPERS

Cut two pounds hot Italian sausages into 2-inch pieces. Place in a shallow baking dish, cover loosely with wax paper and microwave on HIGH for 10 minutes, stirring twice. Remove, uncover, drain well, and discard fat. Add 1 red and 1 green sweet pepper, each stemmed, seeded, and cut into 2-inch chunks, ¼ cup bottled marinara sauce, and 1 teaspoon dried oregano. Cover tightly with plastic wrap and cook on HIGH for 7 minutes. Remove from oven, season with salt, and serve with mashed potatoes. Serves 4.

To make a hero: Split two Italian hero loaves lengthwise, pull out part of the crumb, and pile sausage and peppers into the loaves. Cut each in half. Serves 4.

70 ONION/PEPPER HERO

Seed 1 large green and 1 red bell pepper, and cut into strips. Combine with 1 thinly sliced onion, a few pitted and chopped oil-cured olives, 1 tablespoon olive oil, ½ teaspoon dried thyme, and some chopped garlic (optional). Cover tightly with vented plastic wrap and microwave on HIGH for 6 minutes, stirring once. Let stand covered 2 minutes. Season with salt and pepper and a splash of balsamic vinegar. Spoon into a small Italian loaf sliced in half lengthwise, cut in half, and serve. Serves 2.

71 BLT SALAD

Microwave 2 slices bacon for 45 seconds to one minute on a double layer of paper towels. Remove from oven and let stand 5 minutes. Drain on paper towels and crumble. In a 1-cup glass measure whisk together 1½ tablespoons olive oil, 2 teaspoons wine vinegar, 1 small garlic clove, halved, ¼ teaspoon salt, and fresh black pepper. Heat on MEDIUM-HIGH for 1 minute, until hot. Discard garlic and pour over 6 cups romaine lettuce and 2 large tomatoes, thinly sliced, in a salad bowl. Sprinkle with bacon and serve with buttered whole grain toast. Serves 4.

72 HOT SPICED CIDER

Slice one lemon and one orange thinly. Put a clove in the center of each slice. Combine ½ teaspoon allspice, 2 cinnamon sticks, and 2 tablespoons sugar or to taste in a 3-quart bowl with 2 quarts apple cider and mix well. Add the citrus slices. Microwave on HIGH for 10–15 minutes or until hot and bubbling. Serve warm with a fruit slice or two in each cup. Serves 10.

73 CASSEROLES

When preparing casseroles for the freezer, omit toppings such as grated cheese or bread crumbs, and add at the end after thawing and reheating.

74

Casseroles whose ingredients can be stirred and redistributed will cook most evenly.

75 For even casserole cooking, cut vegetables and meats into fairly uniform sizes and shapes.

76 Let casseroles stand at least 10 minutes after cooking.

77 SOUPS
An easy way to stir soups or other foods in the microwave: use a wooden chopstick or the handle of a wooden spoon, inserted through the vented opening in the plastic.

78 Use potholders when removing soups from the microwave, as the container will get very hot.

79 When reheating a bowl of soup (which can get very hot because of absorbed heat) place on a MWS plate *before* heating, to facilitate removal.

VEGETABLES

80 **GENERAL TIPS**
Add a minimum of water to fresh or frozen vegetables to be microwaved. Extra water slows cooking.

81 Do not add water to fresh vegetables when microwaving. Just rinse in water, but do not shake or dry. The residual moisture is sufficient for most vegetables, and allows more nutrients to be retained.

82 Generally, cut-up vegetables require more cooking liquid. The liquid can be broth or water.

83 If using salt, add at the end of cooking. Salt attracts microwave energy and tends to dehydrate, which can result in tough, overcooked surfaces of tender vegetables.

84 Fresh vegetables microwave best. Test by cutting; moisture should appear on the surface rapidly. If it takes more than a minute to happen (or doesn't occur), add more water.

85 When steaming vegetables which do not require additional moisture, cover tightly **without** venting.

86 **Fibrous vegetables** such as broccoli, asparagus, or artichokes lose texture when reheated.

87 **Moist or starchy vegetables,** such as corn on the cob or a previously baked potato, reheat with a fresh taste when well wrapped in plastic wrap.

88 Do not defrost **frozen vegetables** before cooking them.

89 **BABA GHANOUSH**
Prick a large eggplant (about 1 pound) several times with

a fork, place on double thickness of paper toweling and micro-wave on HIGH, uncovered, for 10–12 minutes or until soft. Place in a colander to cool and drain. In blender or food processor, place 1 small garlic clove, cut up, 2 tablespoons each tahini (sesame paste) and fresh lemon juice, 1 tablespoon olive oil and ½ teaspoon sugar and blend. Split eggplant, scoop out flesh, carefully remove seed sacs, and add to workbowl and puree. Season with salt and pepper to taste and chill half an hour. Garnish with chopped fresh cilantro and serve with toasted pita bread. Makes about 1½ cups.

90 BEANS

Speed soak dried beans (black, kidney, Great Northern, pinto, chick-peas, black-eyed peas). Place 2 cups (1 pound) washed beans in a 4–5-quart casserole with 3 cups hot water or enough to cover. Cover tightly and cook on HIGH for 8–10 minutes or until boiling. Let stand covered, 1 hour. Discard soaking water before cooking.

91

To reheat cooked beans: Use MEDIUM power for 2–3 minutes and either cover with wax paper or leave uncovered. Plastic wrap will cause the skin of cooked beans to rupture from steam buildup.

92 TUSCAN BEANS

Cook 2 cups presoaked Great Northern or cannellini beans, or use canned cooked beans. In a 2-cup glass measure combine 2 tablespoons olive oil and 2–3 minced garlic cloves and 1 teaspoon dried sage or 6 leaves fresh and cook on HIGH for 40 seconds to one minute until garlic is tender. Pass a drained 14-ounce can of tomatoes through a food mill, add and cook on HIGH for 2 minutes. Stir into the cooked drained beans, add salt and fresh black pepper to taste and reheat (p. 41) before serving. Serves 4.

93 STRING BEANS

Combine 1 pound fresh green beans, trimmed, and 2 tablespoons water in a 1½-quart MWS casserole. Cover and microwave on HIGH for 5–6 minutes until beans are crisp-tender. Add 1–2 tablespoons butter and a good squeeze of lemon juice, cover and microwave until butter is melted, 1–2 minutes. Season with salt and pepper, toss to coat evenly and serve. Serves 4–5.

94 LIMA BEAN PUREE

Cook 1 10-ounce box lima beans as directed on package, transfer with any liquid to a food processor and add 2 teaspoons extra-virgin olive oil, ½ teaspoon wine vinegar, ¼ teaspoon oregano, pinch sugar, and salt and pepper to taste and puree. Serves 2.

95 BEETS

Scrub and trim top of 4 medium beets to one inch; leave root stem. Place in a 1-quart casserole with ¼ cup water, cover and vent and cook on HIGH for 12–16 minutes, stirring once. Let stand 5 minutes.

96 HARVARD BEETS

Combine ¼ cup water and 2 tablespoons sugar in a 1-cup glass measure. In a small bowl blend ¼ cup vinegar and 1 tablespoon cornstarch until smooth. Add to the sugar mixture 2 tablespoons butter and salt and pepper to taste and microwave, uncovered, on HIGH for 3–4 minutes until thickened and boiling, stirring twice. Slice 1 pound cooked beets (see above) and combine with sauce in a 1½-quart casserole. Cover tightly and cook on HIGH for 2–3 minutes. Serves 4.

97 QUICK COLD BORSCHT

In a 2-quart MWS bowl, combine 1 fresh 3-inch beet, peeled and coarsely grated (about 1¼ cups), 1 small onion, chopped, 2 tablespoons sugar, and 1½ cups water. Cover tightly and microwave on HIGH for 12–15 minutes, stirring halfway through. Add 2 tablespoons cider vinegar and microwave 3 minutes more. Stir in 1 cup cold water, 2 tablespoons fresh lemon juice, and salt and pepper to taste, and chill. Serve with a dollop of sour cream. For a heartier soup, place a small cold boiled potato in each dish. Serves 2–3.

98 CABBAGE

Remove any unattractive outer leaves from a 1-pound head of green or Savoy cabbage, cut into 4 wedges, arrange in a circle in a glass pie plate with ¼ cup water, cover tightly and cook on HIGH for 12–15 minutes, rearranging wedges once. Let stand covered 3 minutes. Add salt and pepper and 2 tablespoons butter or margarine (optional) and microwave on HIGH for 1 minute to melt butter, if using. Serves 4.

99 BLANCHED CABBAGE LEAVES FOR STUFFING

Cabbage leaves to be stuffed are easier to remove and handle if blanched first. With a sharp knife remove core from cabbage. Place cabbage in a 3-quart casserole with 2 tablespoons water. Cover tightly with plastic wrap and cook on HIGH for 6–8 minutes to blanch leaves. Plunge blanched cabbage into cold water and detach as many large leaves as possible. Pare down thick central rib of each leaf to make rolling easier. Finely chop center of cabbage, add to your favorite stuffing, and proceed with your recipe.

100 SWEET AND SOUR RED CABBAGE

Combine 1 tablespoon each butter and vegetable oil in a 3-quart casserole. Add 1 medium onion, chopped, and cook uncovered on HIGH for 3 minutes, or until onion is tender. Stir in 1 2-pound head of red cabbage, cored and shredded; 1 medium apple, peeled and chopped; 2 tablespoons lemon juice; ¼ cup brown sugar; ½ teaspoon cinnamon; 1 bay leaf; 1 teaspoon salt; several grindings black pepper, and ¼ cup white wine. Cover tightly and cook on HIGH for 10 minutes. Stir, cover, and cook on MEDIUM for 30–40 minutes or until cabbage is tender and the flavors blended. Let stand 5 minutes. Stir in ¼ cup additional white wine and add sugar or seasonings as needed. Remove bay leaf and serve. Serves 4 to 6. Tastes better made a day early and reheated!

101 GLAZED WHOLE BABY CARROTS

Wash 1 pound whole baby carrots. Arrange in a dish just large enough to hold them in two layers, add 2 tablespoons each butter and sugar, cover and microwave on HIGH for 10–12 minutes, stirring gently twice after butter melts. Let stand 3 minutes. Season with salt and pepper. Serves 4.

102 CARROT-PARSNIP PUREE

Scrape a pound each of parsnips and carrots, cut in large dice, and place in a 2-quart MWS casserole with ½ cup water. Microwave on HIGH for 10–15 minutes or until tender, stirring twice. Let stand, covered, for 3 minutes. Put 3 tablespoons butter in a 1-cup measure and microwave on HIGH for

1–2 minutes until melted. Drain and discard liquid from vegetables and puree in a food processor or food mill. Add several gratings nutmeg to the butter and add with some cream or plain yogurt to taste. Season with salt and a dash cayenne. Reheat briefly before serving. Serves 6.

103 CAULIFLOWER WITH CHEESE

Remove stem ends, the core, and any leaves from a medium to large head cauliflower. Rinse but do not shake dry. Place in a MWS dish, cover tightly with plastic wrap and microwave on HIGH for 8–10 minutes or until tender when pierced. Let stand covered 3 minutes. Season lightly, brush top with 2 teaspoons mayonnaise, sprinkle with ½ cup grated Colby or Cheddar cheese and let stand 5 minutes until cheese melts. Cut into wedges to serve. Serves 6.

104 CORN ON THE COB

Shuck 4 ears of corn, rinse, do not dry, place in a zipper-type plastic bag, press out air and microwave on HIGH for 7–8 minutes. Let stand 5 minutes.

105 PRECOOKED CORN FOR THE GRILL

Shorten outdoor grilling time for corn on the cob by microwaving it in the husk. Check tips, remove all but 2 layers of husk, and cook for 2 minutes per ear on HIGH. Fold back husk, butter if desired, pull husk back up, wrap each ear in foil, and place on hot grill for 10–12 minutes.

106 THAI CUCUMBER RELISH

An easy cucumber garnish that is great with spicy food. Microwave ¾ cup rice wine vinegar, ⅓ cup sugar, and a pinch salt, uncovered, in a 2-cup glass measure on HIGH for 3 minutes. Stir until sugar has dissolved. Let cool. In a medium bowl stir together 3 thinly sliced Kirby cucumbers, 3 minced shallots, and 1 seeded and minced jalapeño pepper. Add vinegar mixture and chill. Makes about 2¼ cups.

107 BAKED GARLIC

Slice off the top of a plump head of white garlic, exposing the cloves, and put it in a 2-cup measure with ¼ cup chicken broth and 1 tablespoon of olive oil dribbled over the garlic. Cover tightly with microwave plastic wrap and cook on HIGH for 4 minutes. Let stand 5 minutes. To eat, remove a clove, pull the sweet meat out with the teeth, and eat with crusty country bread as an appetizer or serve as a vegetable with roast chicken.

Add the same amount of broth for two heads, but use a 1½-quart casserole, 2 tablespoons oil and microwave on HIGH for 5 minutes, with 5–10 minutes for standing.

108 PEAS (fresh)
Place 2 cups shelled green peas in a 1½-quart casserole, sprinkle with 2 tablespoons water, cover and vent and microwave on HIGH for 4–6 minutes. Let stand 2 minutes.

109 FRENCH BRAISED PEAS
Separate and wash the leaves of one head Boston lettuce. In a 1½-quart MWS casserole, microwave 2–4 tablespoons butter with 1 tablespoon water until butter melts, about 1½ minutes. Place the lettuce leaves around the bottom and sides of dish, add 1 tablespoon sugar, salt and fresh pepper, and 3 cups shelled fresh peas. Cover and microwave on HIGH for 5–7 minutes until peas are tender, stirring once. Let stand, covered, 5 minutes.

110 SUGAR SNAP OR SNOW PEAS

Cut across stem end of 1 pound peas and pull string off along length of pea. Place 1 pound peas, rinsed but not dried, in a 1½-quart casserole, cover and vent and microwave on HIGH for 2 minutes. Let stand, covered, 3 minutes. Add salt to taste.

111 WINTER SQUASH

Cut in half, needs no additional water to cook, but do cover tightly to retain all available moisture.

112 POTATOES

To bake potatoes: Scrub, pierce with fork, place on double layer of paper towels, 1 inch apart, arranged like spokes of a wheel, thicker end outside. *Standing time:* under an inverted bowl, 5–10 minutes for white potatoes, 3 for sweet potatoes.

113 FOR DRIER BAKED POTATO SKINS

Prick potatoes in several places with a skewer and stand them on end in glass muffin cups while cooking.

Baked Potato Chart

# potatoes	Cooking time
1	4–6 minutes
2	7–8
3	11–13
4	14–16
6	16–18

114 GARLIC MASHED POTATOES

Bake (see chart, above) 4 uniformly medium-size Idaho potatoes, each scrubbed and pricked with a fork, on HIGH for 14–16 minutes. Let stand 5–10 minutes covered with a MWS bowl. Halve lengthwise, scoop out flesh into bowl, mash potatoes with potato masher and reserve. In a small MWS bowl, combine 1 cup milk, 2 tablespoons butter or margarine, 3 cloves minced garlic, and microwave on HIGH for 2 minutes. Mix thoroughly into potatoes. Add additional milk if needed to reach desired consistency, season with salt and pepper and reheat in microwave on HIGH for 1 minute. Sprinkle with chopped parsley and serve immediately. Serves 4.

115 QUICK HOME FRIES

Cut 4 medium scrubbed potatoes (about 1½ pounds) into ¼-inch slices, place in a 2-quart shallow casserole with ¼ cup water, cover tightly and cook on HIGH for 8–10 minutes or until tender, shaking once to redistribute. Let stand covered 2 minutes. Drain, pat dry and pan-fry in a little hot oil about 5–6 minutes, turning with a spatula, until brown and crisp. Season with salt and pepper. Serves 4.

116 OVEN-ROASTED POTATOES

When roasting chicken in the conventional oven, "par-boil" 5 or 6 potatoes, peeled and cut into quarters, with 2 table-spoons water in a MWS casserole in the microwave on HIGH for 13–15 minutes. Drain, place around chicken, baste with pan drippings and roast until browned, about 10–15 minutes.

117 NEW POTATOES

Scrub 1½ pounds small, uniform-size red-skinned new potatoes and peel away a single strip around the middle of each. Place in a 2-quart shallow casserole with 2 tablespoons sweet butter, cut up, cover tightly and microwave on HIGH for 8–10 minutes or until tender, stirring once halfway through. Let stand, covered, 3 minutes. Season to taste. Serves 4.

118 BUTTERED HERBED NEW POTATOES
Prepare potatoes as above. Sprinkle with 2 tablespoons chopped fresh parsley or dill; add salt and fresh pepper to taste and stir to coat well.

119 STEAMED NEW POTATOES
Follow the basic preparation instructions for new potatoes but do not remove a band of peel; simply pierce with a fork and substitute ¼ cup water for the butter. Drain potatoes after cooking and season with salt and freshly ground black pepper.

120 NEW POTATO SALAD
Place 1½ to 2 pounds uniform-size scrubbed red-skinned new potatoes, each pierced with a fork, in a 2-quart casserole with ¼ cup water. Cover tightly and microwave on HIGH for 9–12 minutes, until tender, stirring once to reposition. Let stand, covered, 3 minutes. Drain. When cool enough to han-

dle but still warm, cut in half. In a small bowl combine ¼ cup olive oil, 2 tablespoons vinegar, and salt and pepper to taste. Stir in 1 tablespoon each finely chopped onion and parsley, pour over warm potatoes, mix, and let marinate at least 30 minutes at room temperature. Serves 4–6.

121 SALADE RUSSE

Bake one large potato in the microwave (p. 50). While it cools, microwave 1 box each frozen green peas and frozen lima beans (without butter) according to package directions. Run cold water over and let cool in a colander. Peel and dice the potato and place in a bowl. Add 4–6 medium carrots cut into medium dice, ¼ cup minced onion and the peas and limas. Dress with a sauce made of ⅓ cup mayonnaise, 1 tablespoon lemon juice, and 1 teaspoon sugar. Add a handful of chopped dill and salt and pepper to taste and toss again. Cover tightly and chill before serving. Serves 5–6. Easily doubled for a party.

122 SWEET DUMPLING OR ACORN SQUASH

Cut 2 squash in half around middle, scoop out and discard seeds and strings, add 1 tablespoon brown sugar and a small pat of butter, wrap well and microwave on HIGH for 6–8 minutes, depending on size.

123 MAPLE-BAKED ACORN SQUASH
Follow instructions above, omit brown sugar and add 1 teaspoon maple syrup to each half before cooking.

124 SPAGHETTI SQUASH
Cut squash in half lengthwise and arrange cut side down in a glass baking dish. Pour ¼ cup water around, cover and vent. Microwave on HIGH for 12 minutes or until soft when pressed. Let stand, covered, 3 minutes. Heat your favorite tomato sauce in a bowl, and while squash is warm, scrape flesh with fork to form strands and add to sauce. Toss to combine and sprinkle with grated Parmesan cheese.

125 THAI SPINACH AND GREENS
Stir together 1 tablespoon canola or vegetable oil and 1 minced garlic clove in a MWS round 3-quart casserole with a lid. Cover and microwave covered on HIGH for 2 minutes. Stir in 8 cups washed and dried spinach and/or watercress, the latter

cut into 2-inch lengths. Add ½ small red or green chili pepper, seeded and minced, 1 tablespoon Thai fish sauce (nuoc mam) and ½ teaspoon sugar. Cover with lid and microwave on HIGH for 2–4 minutes, stirring once. Stir thoroughly and let stand, covered, for one minute. Serve hot. Serves 2.

126 WILTED SPINACH WITH SESAME

Tear up 1 pound washed and dried spinach leaves and place in salad bowl. Place 2 tablespoons sesame seeds in a dish and cook on HIGH for 3–4 minutes, stirring twice, until lightly toasted. Let stand 2–3 minutes. In a 2-cup measure combine ¼ cup soy sauce, 2 teaspoons sugar, and 2 tablespoons vegetable oil and cook on HIGH for 1–2 minutes until sugar dissolves. Add sesame seeds to dressing, pour over spinach and toss. Serves 4.

GRAINS

127 BULGHUR WHEAT

Place 1 cup medium bulghur wheat in a 1–2 quart casserole. Microwave 2 cups water or stock on HIGH for 2½ minutes or until boiling, pour over wheat, cover tightly and let stand 20–30 minutes until liquid is absorbed.

128 COUSCOUS

Combine ¾ cup chicken stock or water, 1 teaspoon oil, and ¼ teaspoon salt in a 1-quart casserole. Microwave on HIGH for 2 minutes or until boiling rapidly. Remove from oven and stir in 1 cup instant couscous, cover tightly with lid or plastic wrap and let stand 5 minutes. Fluff lightly with fork before serving. Serves 2.

129 RICE

There is no time advantage to cooking rice in the microwave, but you do get perfect rice every time. To boost flavor, use chicken stock for all or part of the liquid.

130 BROWN RICE

Combine 1 cup brown rice, 2½ cups hot liquid, and 1 teaspoon salt in a round MWS 3-quart casserole. Cover and microwave on HIGH for 5 minutes or until boiling. Reduce power to MEDIUM and cook 25–30 minutes or until liquid is absorbed. Let stand, covered, 5–10 minutes before serving. Makes 3 cups rice, serving 4.

131 LEFTOVER RICE
Freeze leftover rice in 1- and 2-cup quantities. To defrost, place in a 2- or 4-cup casserole and microwave on HIGH for 2–3 minutes for 1 cup, 4–6 minutes for 2, breaking apart and stirring once.

132 WHITE RICE
In a MWS 1-quart casserole combine 1 cup long-grain (Carolina) rice with 2 cups water or broth, 1 tablespoon butter (optional), and ½ teaspoon salt. Cover and cook on HIGH for 5 minutes, lower power to MEDIUM (50%) and cook 15 minutes until liquid is absorbed. DO NOT STIR. Let stand, covered, 5 minutes, fluff with 2 forks and serve. Makes 3 cups cooked rice, serving 4.

Note: A clean dish towel, folded and placed between cover and casserole during standing time, will give you drier, fluffier rice.

133 RICE PILAF
Melt 2 tablespoons butter in a 2-quart casserole, add 1 medium chopped onion and cook uncovered on HIGH for 2–3 minutes until onion is tender, stirring once. Add 1 cup long-grain

rice, stirring well until every grain is coated. Add 1¾ cups chicken broth or stock, stir, cover tightly and cook on HIGH for 4–6 minutes or until liquid is boiling; change setting to MEDIUM and cook 7–10 minutes until most of liquid has been absorbed and rice is tender. Add 1 tablespoon chopped parsley, fluff with 2 forks, cover and let stand 5 minutes. Serves 4.

134 RICE STUFFING WITH CURRANTS AND NUTS

Prepare 1 recipe rice pilaf with ½ cup finely chopped celery added with the onion (p. 58). At end of cooking time combine with ½ cup dried currants, ½ cup chopped pecans, ¼ teaspoon thyme, ½ teaspoon salt and pepper to taste. Makes enough to stuff 4–6 Cornish hens or a 6–7-pound chicken. Bake any leftovers, covered, on HIGH for 1–2 minutes and use as a side dish.

Note: Let stuffing cool if you are planning to stuff birds ahead of time.

135 WILD RICE

Rinse and drain 1 cup wild rice. Combine with 2¼ cups liquid in a 3-quart casserole, cover, and microwave on

HIGH for 5 minutes, change setting to MEDIUM and cook 25–30 minutes or until rice is tender and kernels begin to open. Drain any excess liquid, add salt and pepper to taste and 1 tablespoon butter or margarine. Serves 4.

DRIED STUFF

136 DRIED APPLES
Peel as many apples as you like, core and cut into ¼-inch-thick slices. Make a single layer on a microwave roasting rack and microwave on MEDIUM for 12–15 minutes until limp and moist. Transfer to a wire rack and let stand overnight. Store in a screw-top jar, use in dry cereals.

137 DRIED PORCINI MUSHROOMS
Dried porcini (cepes) are wonderful for risottos and pasta sauces, but very expensive. If you've picked your own or found a bargain at the market, wipe them with a damp paper towel, dry with another, then make thin slices no more than one-eighth-inch thick vertically. Place in a single layer on a double layer of toweling and microwave on HIGH, uncovered, for 3 minutes. Transfer to fresh toweling and microwave 2 minutes on HIGH. Leave on a dry sheet of paper overnight. Store when thor-

oughly dry in a screw-top glass jar. One-half pound of mushrooms will make ¾ cup (about 1 ounce) dried.

138 DRIED HERBS
It is no longer recommended to dry herbs in the microwave as there have been many instances in which they caught on fire.

EGGS

139 FLUFFY SCRAMBLED EGG
In a small MWS bowl, beat together 1 egg and 1 tablespoon milk or water, plus salt and pepper to taste. Microwave uncovered on HIGH for 30 seconds, stir, pulling cooked portions in toward center, and microwave again until egg is just set (30–45 seconds additional). Undercook slightly; egg will continue to cook out of the oven. Serves 1.

140
Use a MEDIUM setting when cooking dishes with a high proportion of eggs.

141 POACHED EGGS

Measure 2 tablespoons water and ¼ teaspoon vinegar into a 6-ounce MWS custard cup. (Use 1 cup per egg.) Microwave on HIGH (45–60 seconds per cup) until water begins to boil. Break an egg into cup, prick yolk with a fork, cover and microwave on MEDIUM until most of the white is opaque but not set, about 30–45 seconds for 1 egg. Remove and let stand 2–3 minutes, shaking cups gently once or twice to help set white. Do not remove cover until standing time is completed. Drain on slotted spoon and place on toasted bread or English muffin.

142 Poached Egg Timing
(Medium—50% power)

1 egg	45 sec. to 1 min. 20 sec.
2 eggs	1 min. 5 sec. to 1 min. 35 sec.
4 eggs	2 min. 15 sec. to 3 min. 15 sec.

Poached egg serving suggestions: Serve on toast, on a bed of cooked spinach, or on top of cooked asparagus.

143 HUEVOS RANCHEROS

Poach 2 eggs as directed above, doubling the amount of vinegar and water. While the eggs are standing, heat 2 tortillas (see below) and reheat a cup of chunky salsa on HIGH for 1 minute. Place a drained poached egg on top of a warm tortilla, spoon salsa over and serve immediately. Serves 2.

144 HEAT FLOUR TORTILLAS

Wrap 4 flour tortillas in a double layer of dampened paper toweling and microwave on HIGH for 30 seconds or until softened and warm to the touch. Let stand for several seconds before using. Do not overheat tortillas or they will become brittle.

MEAT

145 GROUND MEAT

Shape ground meat into a donut shape with a hole in the center before freezing; it will defrost more quickly and evenly.

146 **LAMB CURRY**
In a 3-quart casserole combine 2 tablespoons vegetable oil, 1 cup chopped onion, 2 cloves minced garlic, ½ cup each chopped apple and chopped celery, cover tightly and cook on HIGH for 3–5 minutes, or until tender. Add 2 cups or more leftover roast lamb cut into 1-inch cubes to the vegetables, sprinkle with 2 tablespoons flour and ¼ cup curry powder, cover and cook on HIGH for 10 minutes until little pink remains, stirring after 5 minutes to redistribute meat. Add 1 cup each diced peeled tomatoes and chicken broth and salt and pepper to taste, cover again and cook on HIGH for 7–10 minutes or until boiling. Stir in ½ cup plain yogurt and let stand, covered, 5 minutes. Serve with white rice, made earlier and reheated, and accompany with chutney. Serves 4.

147 With uncooked lamb: Increase second cooking of meat to 20 minutes, and standing time to 10 minutes.

148 **QUICK GYROS**
In a 1-quart casserole combine a tablespoon butter or olive oil, 1 medium sliced onion, and a minced garlic clove. Cook on HIGH for 2–4 minutes until onion is tender. Stir in ¾ pound

sliced leftover lamb, ¼ teaspoon oregano and salt and pepper to taste. Cover with wax paper and cook on HIGH for 2 minutes or until heated through, stirring once. Spoon into pita pockets with lettuce and tomato and Cucumber-Yogurt Sauce if desired (below). Serves 4.

Cucumber-Yogurt Sauce

Put 2 cups plain yogurt in a cheesecloth-lined sieve in a bowl and let drain for 3 hours. Peel, seed, and chop 2 cucumbers very finely, sprinkle with salt and set aside for 1 hour to drain. Combine yogurt, 2 tablespoons olive oil, 1 tablespoon fresh lemon juice, and 2–5 cloves minced garlic. Refrigerate. Just before serving, beat with a wooden spoon and add the cucumber, squeezed dry, and ¼ cup torn-up fresh mint leaves or coarsely chopped flat-leaf parsley and salt and pepper to taste. Serve as an hors d'oeuvre, salad, or stuffed in a pita.

149 BARBECUED STEAK

For the one-in-every-crowd who wants a well-done steak, grill all steaks as you do normally, then microwave requests for well-done in the microwave. Prevents overly charring meat, too.

Those concerned with decreasing the risk of colorectal cancer are advised by experts to microwave meats for 1 minute and remove the juices formed, before cooking by any other method.

POULTRY

150 CHICKEN

When you need cooked chicken for a recipe, such as chicken salad, place 2½ pounds cut-up chicken, skin side up, in a 10-inch shallow MWS casserole or pie plate. Add ½ cup water, cover with wax paper and microwave on HIGH for 9–12 minutes. Let stand 5 minutes, then remove skin and bones and cut into bite-size pieces.

151 BARBECUED CHICKEN

Place a washed and dried cut-up 3-pound chicken, skin side down, in a rectangular MWS dish. Cover with wax paper and cook on HIGH for 6 minutes per pound. Turn chicken and rearrange once during cooking. Brush with Barbecue Sauce (p. 70) and grill on a preheated, oiled grill for 10 minutes, turning once. Chicken will be moist within, nicely crisped outside.

152 CHICKEN BREASTS

Arrange 2 whole chicken breasts (4 pieces) split, boned, and skinned in a 10-inch glass pie plate with thicker portion toward outside of dish. Drizzle with 2–3 tablespoons chicken broth, cover with a MWS dinner plate or wax paper and microwave on HIGH for 4 minutes. Turn breasts, cover again and microwave on MEDIUM for 3–4 minutes more, or until just springy to the touch. Let stand 5 minutes.

153 SUMMER CHICKEN

Place 4 cooked boneless breasts (see above) on serving plates, top with drained Thai Cucumber Relish (p. 48) and sprinkle with 2 tablespoons chopped fresh cilantro. Serve at room temperature. Serves 4.

154 CHICKEN LIVERS

Livers can be tricky to defrost as it is easy to accidentally cook them in their own juices. Defrost a 1-pound package on HIGH for 2 minutes; remove livers from package and put on a MWS rack in a glass dish or casserole. Reset to MEDIUM for 2–3 minutes, then gently separate livers and arrange any still icy portions toward outside of dish and pour off any liquid that has formed. Reset again to DEFROST (MEDIUM-LOW) for 4–5 minutes per pound. Let stand 5 minutes then pat dry with paper towel before cooking.

155 THAWING POULTRY

Salmonella poisoning from poultry has been on the rise in the last two decades; use the microwave for thawing only if you plan to cook poultry right away; if not, re-refrigerate until cooking time to avoid the multiplication of bacteria.

156 TO DEFROST POULTRY

Microwave for 4 minutes per pound at DEFROST (MEDIUM-LOW). Let stand in the refrigerator for at least 1 hour before cooking.

When defrosting Cornish game hens, place breast side down and turn halfway through defrosting. Rinse hens inside and out and let stand 15 minutes before cooking.

When microwaving cut-up chicken, place meatiest parts toward the outside, bony parts toward the center.

157 CHICKEN TONNATO

Cook 4 boneless breasts (p. 67) on HIGH for 7–10 minutes. Let cool. Line a serving platter with romaine lettuce leaves, arrange chicken on top and mask with half the tuna sauce (below), decorated with 1 tablespoon drained capers and tomato and lemon slices around the edges. Pass remaining sauce.

158 TUNA SAUCE

In a food processor or blender combine 1 7-ounce can Italian tuna in olive oil, drained, with 5 flat anchovy fillets, ½ cup olive oil, and 3 tablespoons lemon juice. Remove and fold carefully into 1 cup mayonnaise. Taste to see if salt is needed, and refrigerate until ready to serve.

159 GLAZED STUFFED CORNISH HENS

Rinse 4 1-pound Cornish hens, pat dry and season inside and out. Stuff with favorite stuffing or Rice Stuffing with Currants and Nuts (p. 59). Truss and place breast side down in a 10-inch round shallow MWS baking dish with drumsticks toward center. Brush with half of Quick Glaze (p. 70) and cook, uncovered, on HIGH for 16 minutes. Turn and brush with remaining

---

glaze and cook on HIGH for 16–22 minutes, or until juices run clear. Tent with foil and let stand 5 minutes before serving.

Tip: You can get an attractive deeper brown hen if you run the baking dish under a broiler with rack set at lowest position for 25–30 seconds ONLY. Keep door ajar and watch carefully so birds do not burn.

160 QUICK GLAZE FOR CORNISH HENS
Place 2 tablespoons butter in a 1-cup glass measure and cook on HIGH for 40–65 seconds until melted. Stir in 1 tablespoon each honey and soy sauce. Enough for roasting 4 birds. Adds lovely color, too.

SAUCES

161 When making a sauce that needs stirring 2 or 3 times during cooking, use a 2- or 4-cup measure and a plastic or wooden spoon that can be left in place during cooking. Saves time, will not get hot, and eliminates drips.

162 BARBECUE SAUCE FOR CHICKEN
In a 4-cup glass measure combine 1 cup tomato cat-

sup, ¼ cup cider or wine vinegar, 2 tablespoons prepared mustard, 2 tablespoons chili powder, ½ cup brown sugar, 2 tablespoons Worcestershire sauce, 1 tablespoon soy sauce, 2 tablespoons vegetable oil, and freshly ground pepper. Blend well and microwave on HIGH for 5–7 minutes or until boiling, stirring after 2 minutes.

163 QUICK TOMATO SAUCE WITH BASIL

Place the contents of 1 28-ounce can crushed Italian plum tomatoes, 3 tablespoons olive oil, 4 cloves minced garlic, 2 teaspoons salt and freshly ground pepper in a 2-quart Pyrex baking dish and microwave, uncovered, on HIGH for 6 minutes. Remove from oven and stir in 1 tablespoon tomato paste and 2 tablespoons shredded fresh basil. Cook, uncovered, on HIGH for 3 minutes.

164 CRANBERRY SAUCE MOLD

Combine 1 bag (12 ounces) fresh or frozen cranberries with 1 cup granulated sugar and ½ cup cranberry juice in an 8-cup glass measure. Cook, uncovered, on HIGH for 10 minutes. Remove from oven and stir. Rinse a 2-quart mold or soufflé dish with cold water, pour in cranberry sauce and refrigerate, loosely covered, for 4–6 hours. Unmold onto a serving platter.

165 GARLIC BUTTER

Handy for making garlic bread: combine 1 stick sweet butter, cut up, 2 minced garlic cloves, and a tablespoon chopped parsley in a 2-cup glass measure, cover with wax paper and microwave on HIGH for 1½ minutes until butter is melted and garlic is tender. Add salt to taste. Makes about ½ cup.

166 GRAVY

For easy, lump-free gravy: During cooking, collect drippings from your turkey or roast in a 4-cup MWS measure. Let stand so fat can rise to surface and be skimmed off. Microwave skimmed drippings on HIGH (1–4 minutes, depending on amount) until boiling. Meanwhile, in a small bowl combine 1 tablespoon thickener (flour, cornstarch, or arrowroot) and 1 tablespoon liquid (water, broth, cream) for each cup drippings. Rapidly stir this into hot drippings, mixing well. Microwave on HIGH for 1–3 minutes until gravy boils and thickens, stirring every minute. Season to taste with salt, fresh pepper and add some red wine or Madeira if desired.

167 HEALTHFUL HOLLANDAISE SAUCE
Beat 3 large egg yolks lightly and reserve. In a MWS 1-quart glass measure or bowl microwave ½ stick (4 tablespoons) butter on HIGH for 1 minute or until melted, then whisk in ¼ cup half-and-half, the egg yolks, 1 tablespoon lemon juice, ½ teaspoon dry mustard, salt to taste, and a pinch of cayenne. Microwave on HIGH for 1 minute, whisk vigorously and cook on HIGH for 45 seconds or until sauce registers 150° on an instant-read thermometer. Whisk once more. Makes about ¾ cup.

168 RED PEPPER SAUCE
Put 1 teaspoon vegetable oil and 1 sweet red pepper, seeded and cut into 4 pieces, in a 1-quart glass bowl, cover and microwave on HIGH for 2 minutes. Add ½ cup defatted chicken stock, stir and microwave 1 minute. Puree in a food processor or blender until smooth. Strain through a fine sieve into same glass measure and microwave on MEDIUM for 1 minute. Season to

taste with salt and pepper. Makes 1¼ cups, enough to accompany grilled fish for 2. May be made ahead, refrigerated, and reheated.

169 BLUEBERRY SAUCE

Using a fork, crush a handful of blueberries from a picked-over pint in the bottom of a 4-cup glass measure. Add the remaining berries, sprinkle with 3 tablespoons granulated sugar, cover tightly with plastic wrap and cook on HIGH for 3 minutes. Put through a food mill. Add a dash cinnamon and 2 tablespoons Cointreau or Triple Sec and additional sugar as needed. Serve warm. Makes 1½ cups. For ice cream, pancakes, waffles.

For a chunkier sauce, prepare as above, but do not put through food mill.

SEAFOOD

170

When cooking fish in the microwave, check it after the minimum time has elapsed, as fish will continue to cook in its own heat: part fish with a knife tip at its thickest point; it should no longer be translucent, but should not readily flake.

171 Another way to check fish for doneness: Insert a metal skewer in the thickest part of the flesh. Leave for about 2 seconds and apply to your inner arm or lower lip. It should feel very warm; if uncomfortably hot, the fish is overdone.

172 Fish fillets should be cooked on the smallest dishes or plates on which they can fit in a single layer. If the fillets have skin, make 2 or 3 slashes across the width so fish does not curl.

173 You can cook any fish with just 1 or 2 teaspoons of liquid and eliminate fat entirely. If you do want it for flavor, drizzle a spoonful of olive oil or melted butter over fish after cooking and just before serving—the oil will taste fresher and stronger than if cooked.

174 Fish will continue to cook if left wrapped and can easily become overdone. Unless recipe specifies otherwise, unwrap immediately after cooking or pierce plastic with a knife to let steam escape.

175 When preparing a meal around microwaved fish fillets, cook these last and serve immediately. If vegetables cool off, they are easier to reheat.

176 Leaving in bones and skin will not affect cooking times for fish fillets and steaks.

177 One fillet half an inch thick and weighing 6–8 ounces will cook in 2–3½ minutes on HIGH; 2 pieces will take 2½–4 minutes.

178 It is easy to overcook thin fish fillets, especially the thinner end, when they are laid flat. Tuck thinner ends under the thicker middle portion for protection, or roll fillets.

179 **FLOUNDER OR SOLE FILLETS**
Fold or roll 1 pound of fillets as described above and place around the perimeter of a round MWS dish and sprinkle with lemon juice. Loosely cover with a paper towel and microwave on HIGH for 2½–4 minutes or until fish is completely

opaque. Drain off accumulated liquid, cover again with the towel and let stand 2 minutes. Serve with Lemon Butter or top with Buttered Crumbs (below).

180 LEMON BUTTER FOR FISH
Place 4 tablespoons butter in a glass measure, microwave on HIGH for 1 minute to melt and stir in 1 tablespoon lemon juice.

181 BUTTERED BREAD CRUMBS FOR FISH
Make Lemon Butter (above) and add ¼ cup fine dry bread crumbs (p. 87) after the lemon juice.

Individual serving: 1 tablespoon butter and 2 teaspoons lemon juice or 1 tablespoon dry bread crumbs.

182 ORIENTAL FLOUNDER FILLETS
Arrange a pound of flounder fillets in a large round MWS baking dish that can go to the table; season with salt and pepper, cover with plastic wrap and microwave on HIGH for 3 minutes or until opaque. Remove wrap, pour off liquid in dish

and cover loosely with foil. In a 1-cup glass measure combine 2 tablespoons vegetable oil, 1 tablespoon grated or finely julienned ginger root, and 1 large julienned scallion and microwave on HIGH for 1 minute. Add 1 teaspoon dark sesame oil. Let cool slightly, pour over fish and serve sprinkled with soy sauce to taste. A splash of rice vinegar is lovely. Serves 2 to 3.

183 MUSSELS MARINIÈRE

In a 3-quart casserole combine 2 tablespoons butter, 2 minced garlic cloves, ¼ cup finely minced onion, and cook on HIGH for 35 seconds to 1 minute to melt butter. Stir in 1 cup dry white wine, a small bay leaf, a pinch of thyme, and several grindings black pepper. Cover tightly and cook on HIGH for 5 minutes. Add 3 pounds scrubbed mussels, unshelled, cover tightly and cook on HIGH for 5–7 minutes until mussels have opened, stirring every 2 minutes to rearrange. Transfer mussels that open wide to a bowl and keep warm. Let stand, covered, 2 minutes. Discard any unopened mussels. Serve in soup bowls, sprinkled with chopped parsley. Crusty bread is a must with this. Serves 4.

184 SALMON TERIYAKI

Place 4 salmon steaks, about ½ inch thick (about 2 pounds), in a shallow ungreased 2-quart MWS baking dish with tails toward the center. In a cup combine 2 tablespoons light soy sauce, 1 tablespoon sherry, 1 teaspoon lemon juice, 1½ teaspoons sugar, and a crushed garlic clove, pour over the fish and let marinate at room temperature for ½ hour. Cover tightly with plastic wrap and microwave on HIGH for 7 minutes. Let stand, covered, 2–3 minutes, then sprinkle with 2 finely sliced scallions (white and part of the green). Serve with rice.

Cook two steaks for 4–4½ minutes, but use the same amount of marinade.

185 SHRIMP IN GARLIC BUTTER

In a 3-quart MWS casserole microwave 4 tablespoons butter on MEDIUM until melted. Add 4 large garlic cloves, put through a press, a tablespoon each lemon juice and minced parsley, and 1 pound peeled medium or large shrimp (deveined also if you like) arranged in a single layer around perimeter of dish. Microwave on HIGH for 3–4 minutes until shrimp are pink, stirring once halfway through cooking to move uncooked shrimp to outside of dish. Let stand 1 minute. Season with salt and pepper and serve over rice. Garnish with lemon wedges. Serves 4.

186 *Note:* Never deep-fry fish in the microwave.

DESSERTS

187 **BAKED APPLES**
Core 4 Granny Smith apples without cutting all the way through, and enlarge opening. Peel top third of each. In a bowl combine ¼ cup each chopped walnuts and light brown sugar with ½ teaspoon cinnamon, dash nutmeg, 1 tablespoon softened butter, and a splash of rum, and spoon into each apple. Place apples, not touching, in a deep 2½-quart MWS baking dish and pour ⅓ cup orange juice over apples. Cover with plastic wrap and microwave on HIGH for 6 minutes. Pierce wrap with the tip of a sharp knife and let stand covered 5 minutes. (Apples will continue to steam.) Uncover and serve warm with the syrup spooned over.

188 BAKED APPLE WITH CRÈME ANGLAISE

For a fancy dessert, prepare Crème Anglaise (p. 83) and spoon onto the center of the plate, making a smooth circle with the back of the spoon, and set the baked apple on top.

189 APPLE CRUMBLE

Put 4 cups peeled, cored, and thinly sliced apples in a 9-inch glass pie plate. In a mixing bowl combine ½ cup brown sugar with 1 teaspoon cinnamon and a dash of nutmeg and sprinkle over apples. Add 1 tablespoon lemon juice and grated zest of 1 orange. In another bowl combine ⅓ cup brown sugar with ½ cup each flour and rolled oats; cut in 2 tablespoons butter until mixture is crumbly. Sprinkle evenly over apples. Microwave on HIGH for 12–14 minutes, or until fruit is tender. Let stand 3 minutes. If a browner top is desired, run under the broiler. Serve warm. Serves 6.

190 BUTTERSCOTCH PUDDING

Melt 4 tablespoons butter, uncovered, in a 2-quart round glass casserole on HIGH for about 1 minute. Whisk in ¾ cup packed dark brown sugar and microwave on HIGH for 1 minute until boiling. Whisk in 1 cup half-and-half until smooth. In a small bowl stir together 2 tablespoons cornstarch until dissolved. Add with remaining ½ cup half-and-half and a pinch salt to sugar mixture and whisk in. Microwave uncovered on HIGH for 5–6 minutes until thickened, whisking every 2 minutes. Remove from oven and whisk until smooth. Whisk in 1 teaspoon vanilla extract, place in 4 serving dishes and chill. Garnish with coarsely chopped toasted pecans if desired. Serves 4.

191 PEACH CRUMBLE

Substitute thinly sliced ripe peaches for the apples in Apple Crumble (p. 81) and microwave on HIGH for 8–10 minutes.

192 STEWED PRUNES AND APRICOTS

Combine 1 cup water, 1 tablespoon sugar, and a dash of vanilla extract in a 1-quart glass casserole and stir. Add 1 cup each dried prunes and apricots and 2 or 3 curls of lemon zest, cover tightly and microwave on HIGH for 5–6 minutes. Let stand 5 minutes. Cool and chill. Use as a dessert or a relish. Serves 3.

193 STEWED RHUBARB AND STRAWBERRIES

In a 3-quart MWS bowl combine 4 cups sliced fresh rhubarb with ¼ cup orange juice and ¾ cup sugar or more to taste, cover and vent and microwave on HIGH for 8–10 minutes, stirring halfway through. Stir in 1 cup hulled and sliced strawberries, cover again and let stand until cool. Chill. Serves 6.

194 CRÈME ANGLAISE

Whisk together 3 egg yolks and 2 tablespoons sugar in a medium bowl. Heat 1 cup milk in a 4-cup glass measure, uncovered, on HIGH for 1½ minutes. Remove from oven and whisk 2 or 3 tablespoonfuls into the egg mixture to warm it, then add egg mixture to the remaining heated milk. Cook, uncovered, on MEDIUM for 4–5 minutes or until it thickens and coats the back of a spoon, stirring 2 or 3 times. Whisk in ½ teaspoon vanilla extract, strain sauce into a clean bowl and chill, tightly covered. Makes 1¼ cups. Use with poached or fresh fruits, gingerbread, baked apple, or apple crisp.

195 GRAHAM CRUMB PIE SHELL

In a food processor process 18 crushed single graham crackers, 3 tablespoons brown sugar, ½ teaspoon cinnamon, and

6 tablespoons butter or margarine, cut up. With your hand, press into the bottom and sides of a 9-inch glass pie plate. Microwave, uncovered, on HIGH for 2 minutes or until set, giving plate a quarter-turn after 1 minute if you have no turntable.

196 CHOCOLATE WAFER SHELL
Follow Graham Crumb Pie Shell recipe (p. 83) but use 28–30 crushed chocolate wafer cookies.

197 FRUIT TART GLAZE
You can melt jelly in the microwave to glaze a fruit tart. Push jelly through a strainer if it contains bits of whole fruit and heat on HIGH for 1–2 minutes until slightly bubbly. Brush over tart with a pastry brush. If jelly thickens, heat again.

FOOD KIDS CAN MAKE

198 PEPPERONI PIZZA CRACKERS
Place 4 saltine crackers on a glass or paper plate, spread with bottled pizza sauce, top each with one fourth of a slice of mozzarella cheese and a thin slice of pepperoni. Microwave at MEDIUM for 30–60 seconds until cheese melts.

199 HAMBURGER

Place a quarter-pound hamburger on a microwave roasting rack. Cover with wax paper and microwave on HIGH for 1 minute. Turn burger and cover again; microwave 30 seconds to 1 minute more, depending on degree of doneness desired. Let stand 1–2 minutes.

200

Two patties: Cook first side for 1½ minutes; second side for 1–2 minutes.

201 CHOCOLATE CRISPY CLUSTERS

Distribute 6 ounces semisweet chocolate pieces in a circle in a 1-quart casserole, leaving the center bare. Cook on MEDIUM for 2 minutes; stir, cook 30 seconds to 1½ minutes more, stirring every 30 seconds. Remove from oven and stir in 2 cups Rice Krispies and mix well to coat. Spoon rounded teaspoons of mixture onto a wax paper–lined cookie sheet and refrigerate to harden.

202 HOMEMADE CHOCOLATE PUDDING
In an 8-cup MWS measuring cup or bowl blend together ½ cup sugar, ¼ cup Dutch-process cocoa, 3 tablespoons cornstarch, and a dash of salt. Gradually whisk in 2¼ cups milk. Microwave, uncovered, on HIGH for 6–7 minutes, stirring every 2 minutes, until thickened and boiling. Add 1 teaspoon vanilla extract. Put a piece of wax paper on top so a skin doesn't form, let cool and then chill. Serves 4.

203 CHOCOLATE CREAM PIE
Make a Chocolate Wafer Shell (p. 84). Pour cooked Homemade Chocolate Pudding (above) into it, chill and serve plain or decorated with whipped cream.

204 POPCORN: See instructions pp. 18, 30.
See also: Baked Potato (p. 50), Baked Apples (p. 80), Snacks (pp. 33–38), Butterscotch Pudding (p. 81), Heating Soup (p. 31), Creamy Oatmeal (p. 88), Scrambled Egg (p. 61), Baking Tips (pp. 89–91)

MISCELLANEOUS

205 QUICK APPLE BUTTER

In a 3-quart Pyrex casserole with a lid, stir together 6 cups (about 2¾ pounds) tart, flavorful apples, peeled, cored, and cut in 1-inch chunks and ¾ cup unsweetened apple cider. Cover and microwave on HIGH for 8–11 minutes, until very soft, stirring every 3 minutes. Puree apples in food processor or blender in 2 batches. Return to same casserole, add 1 teaspoon grated lemon rind, ½ cup brown sugar, ¼ teaspoon ground cinnamon, and a pinch each ground cloves, allspice, and salt. Microwave uncovered on HIGH for about 20 minutes until very thick, stirring every 4 minutes, checking consistency. If needed, cook longer, checking and stirring after each minute.

For immediate use, cool and refrigerate. Will last for a month or more. Or process in sealed jars in a water bath as you would preserves. Makes 2½ pints.

206 HOMEMADE BREAD CRUMBS

Trim and discard crusts from about one-half pound French or Italian bread or home-style white bread. Crumble by hand or briefly in a food processor. Spread in a thin layer in a 9- or 10-inch pie plate or similar dish and microwave, uncovered, on HIGH for 8 minutes, stirring twice during cooking. Remove from oven and cool. If very fine crumbs are needed, whirl again in the food processor. Store tightly covered. Makes about ¾ cup.

207 CREAMY OATMEAL WITH RAISINS
This "creamy" version is low in fat and has no cream! In a 2-cup glass measure combine ⅓ cup of old-fashioned rolled oats with a dash of salt, 2 tablespoons raisins, and ¾ cup skim milk. Cook on MEDIUM for 5–6 minutes, stir and let stand 3 minutes. Sprinkle with cinnamon sugar if desired. Serves 1.

208 SIMPLE SYRUP
This sweetener dissolves instantly and is great for iced tea, mixed drinks and punches, and making sorbets. In an 8-cup glass measure combine 2 cups sugar and 2 cups water, stirring to mix. Cover tightly and microwave on HIGH for 8–10 minutes until mixture boils and becomes clear. Remove carefully using potholders; handle will be hot. Cool syrup and store covered in a glass jar in the refrigerator. Will keep refrigerated at least six months. Makes 1 quart.

MORE BAKING TIPS

209 Cake flour will give a better texture and lighter cake. To substitute for all-purpose flour, increase the amount by 2–3 tablespoons for each cup of flour.

210 Don't bake cakes that use only egg whites in the microwave; they don't do as well as whole-egg cakes.

211 A one-layer cake recipe will make a 9 inch round or an 8 × 8 square cake in the microwave.

212 A cake dish to be microwaved should be filled no more than one-third to one-half full. If you have leftover batter, make 2 or 3 cupcakes in 5- or 6-ounce Pyrex custard cups.

213 A two-layer recipe may be made in a 14-cup microwave ring or Bundt pan, but do check the pan's capacity. If it is a 12-cup pan, follow the filling suggestion above and make 2 or 3 cupcakes with remaining batter.

214 Elevate cakes on a MWS rack, cereal dish, inverted Pyrex pie plate for more even baking.

215 For best results when baking cakes in the microwave, let batter sit in pan 5 minutes *before* baking. This gives gluten time to relax before being exposed to rapid heat, making a lighter cake.

216 Standing time is important in cake baking because it allows the center to complete cooking. Remove cake from oven when it has just pulled away from the sides and is still slightly moist on top. Cover tightly with foil and let stand directly on the counter for 10 minutes. A toothpick should test clean in several places.

217 The bottom of a microwaved cake is the last part to completely cook and this is usually completed during standing time. For this reason do not place cake on the usual wire rack but rather on the counter to trap as much heat as possible.

If after the 10-minute standing period you invert the cake and there still appears to be raw batter on the bottom, put the cake back in on MEDIUM for an additional minute; check and repeat as necessary.

218 Rotate baking dish once or twice during cooking, so cake will rise uniformly. Do this even if you have a turntable.

219 Since microwave cakes have a more fragile texture, make frostings a bit thinner; apply a light layer, let set, then add remaining frosting.

HIGH ALTITUDE MICROWAVING

At high elevations thinner air and lower air pressure affect microwave cooking as they do conventional cooking.

220 DISHES
Use larger dishes in high altitudes, as foods tend to expand and bubble more.

221 **COOKING TIMES**
Increase cooking time slightly, as foods do not get as hot due to the lower boiling point. When instructions give a range of times the longer time is usually needed.

222 **Soups** are cooked covered. **Sauces** are cooked uncovered so they will thicken.

223 **BAKED PRODUCTS**
Select recipes designed for microwaving; they need less adjustment than conventional ones.

224 Cakes and breads rise higher, are more crumbly, and can even fall due to excess leavening action.

225 Baked products tend to be drier, because of the drier atmosphere, so use the large or jumbo eggs when baking.

226 Finely chop nuts and fruits with flour so they will be well distributed through batter.

227 For boxed cake mixes: If high altitude microwave directions aren't given, watch baking time and add 1–2 minutes if cake falls; elevate from floor of oven if bottom isn't well cooked.

228 If cake from a mix is too crumbly, add 1 extra tablespoon flour the next time.

INDEX

ABOUT THE AUTHOR

Ruth Spear is a journalist and food writer whose articles on food, health, and travel have appeared in *New York, Travel & Leisure, Food & Wine, Cuisine, Bon Appetit, Diversion, Woman's Day, Good Housekeeping, The Ladies' Home Journal, Cosmopolitan, Harper's Bazaar, Good Food, The Pleasures of Cooking,* and *Eating Well* magazines.

A food columnist for the *New York Post* and the author of several cookbooks, including *Cooking Fish and Shellfish, The Classic Vegetable Cookbook, What Can I Do with My Microwave?,* and *Low Fat and Loving It,* Ruth Spear lives with her husband and two daughters in New York City and East Hampton.